Raise Your Glasses

Raise Your Glasses

The best and wittiest anecdotes and
after-dinner stories from the famous

Collected by
PHYLLIS
SCHINDLER

PIATKUS

This compilation of stories and anecdotes by distinguished people, will, I hope, be of assistance to potential after-dinner speakers and will also amuse the reader. I hope, too, that St. Bartholomew's Hospital Children's Cancer Ward will greatly benefit from the royalties.

My thanks to all the contributors who took the time and trouble to make this book possible.

Copyright © 1988 by Phyllis Shindler

First published in Great Britain in 1988 by
Piatkus Books Ltd of
5 Windmill Street, London W1T 2JA
info@piatkus.co.uk

Reprinted six times

This edition published in 2004

The moral right of the author has been asserted

A catalogue record for this book is available from the British Library

ISBN 0-7499-2539-6

Illustrations by Ellis Nadler
Typeset in 11/13pt Linotron Palatino by
Phoenix Photosetting, Lordswood, Chatham, Kent
Printed and bound in Great Britain by
Mackay of Chatham Ltd, Chatham, Kent

Contributors

Foreword by Sir Angus Ogilvy 9

The Rt. Hon. The Lord
Aberdare 11

Dannie Abse 12

Arthur R. Ashe 13

Vladimir Ashkenazy 14

A 'Musical Friend' 16

Nina Bawden 18

Margaret A. Boden 19

The Rt. Hon. Lord Boyd-
Carpenter 21

Katie Boyle 22

The Rt. Hon. The Lord
Brandon of Oakbrook 23

Gyles Brandreth 24

The Rt. Hon. Viscountess
Bridgeman 25

B. J. Brown 27

Helen Gurley Brown 28

General Sir Edward
Burgess 29

The Rt. Hon. Lord Carr of
Hadley 30

The Rt. Hon. Lord
Carrington 32

Sir Hugh Casson 33

Alderman John
Chalstrey 34

His Excellency Mr. Ji
Chaozho, The Ambassador
of the People's Republic of
China 35

The Rt. Hon. Lord
Charteris of Amisfield 36

The Rt. Hon. Lord
Cledwyn of Penrhos 37

Sir Colin Cole 38

Lady Georgina
Coleridge 39

Sir Kenneth Cork 40

M. Colin Cowdrey 42

Wendy Craig 43

The Rt. Hon. The Lord
Cudlipp 44

The Rt. Hon. Baron
Delfont of Stepney 46

The Rt. Hon. Viscount de
L'Isle 47

The Rt. Hon. Lord
Denham 48

Kirk Douglas 49

The Rt. Hon. Sir Edward
du Cann 50

The Very Reverend R.M.S.
Eyre 51

The Lord Fanshaw 52

Bryan Forbes 53

Sir Vivian Fuchs 55

G.W.H. Gibbs 56

Sir John Gielgud 58

Rumer Godden 59

Sir Arthur Gold 60

Lord Grade 61

Beryl Grey 61

James Herriot 62

The Rt. Hon. Lord Holderness 63

Lady Holland-Martin 64

The Rt. Hon. Sir Geoffrey Howe 65

Gloria Hunniford 66

Sir Leonard Hutton 67

Jeremy Irons 68

Elizabeth Jenkins 69

Howel Jones 70

Sir John Junor 71

The Rt. Hon. Lord Justice Kerr 72

The Lord Killearn 73

Dame Jill Knight 74

Sir Larry Lamb 75

John le Carré 76

Jan Leeming 78

The Rt. Hon. Viscount Leverhulme of the Western Isles 80

The Lord Lloyd of Kilgerran 81

Christopher Logue 82

The Rt. Hon. The Countess of Longford 83

The Rt. Hon. The Earl of Longford 84

Admiral Sir Raymond Lygo 85

The Rt. Hon. The Lord Mackay of Clashfern 87

The Rt. Hon. Lord Marshall of Leeds 88

His Excellency The Hon. Mr. Douglas McClelland, The Australian High Commissioner 89

His Excellency Mr. Roy McMurtry, The Canadian High Commissioner 90

Sir Yehudi Menuhin 91

Lady Mills (Mary Hayley Bell) 92

Sheridan Morley 93

Malcolm Muggeridge 94

The Rt. Rev. Peter Mumford 95

His Excellency Señor Navarrete, The Mexican Ambassador 96

Sir Angus Ogilvy 97

The Rt. Hon. Sir Michael Palliser 98

His Excellency Mr. Ilkka Pastinen, The Finnish Ambassador 99

The Rt. Hon. The Lord Ponsonby of Shulbrede 100

His Excellency Mr. Charles H. Price II, The United States Ambassador 101

The Rt. Hon. Lord Prior 102

Steve Race 103

Ronald Reagan 105

The Lord Renton 109

Brian Rix 110

Samuel Sheppard 111

The Rt. Hon. Sir Greville Spratt 112

Sir Sigmund Sternberg 113

The Rt. Hon. Earl of Stockton 114

The Rt. Rev. Mervyn Stockwood 115

Godfrey Talbot 116

His Excellency Dr. Reginald Thomas 120

The Rt. Hon. The Baroness Trumpington of Sandwich 121

His Honour Judge Stephen Tumim 122

Alan Whicker 124

Mrs. Mary Whitehouse 125

Colin Wilson 127

The Rt. Hon. The Lady Wilson of Rievaulx 128

Foreword
by Sir Angus Ogilvy

It is desperately difficult to find after-dinner stories which have not been told often before. *Raise Your Glasses* does, however, contain a unique and amusing collection – most of which I personally have never heard before.

It has been compiled by Phyllis Shindler and thanks to her generosity all the royalties will go to the Children's Cancer Ward at St. Bartholomew's Hospital. Successful treatment of this dreaded disease is unfortunately dependent upon the use of highly sophisticated and costly equipment.

It would be hard to find a more worthwhile cause than one which enables children to survive who would otherwise have died.

Thank you for your support.

Angus Ogilvy.

The Rt. Hon. The Lord Aberdare

K.B.E., P.C.

Chairman of Committees, House of Lords, Author

The Bureaucrat's Hymn

O Thou, who seest all things below,
Grant that Thy servants may go slow,
That they may study to comply
With regulations, till they die.

Teach us, Lord, to reverence,
Committees more than commonsense,
Impress our minds to make no plan,
But pass the baby when we can.

And when the tempter seems to give
Us feelings of initiative,
Or when, alone, we go too far,
Chastise us with a circular.

Mid war and tumult, fire and storms,
Strengthen us, we pray, with forms.
Thus will Thy servants ever be
A Flock of perfect sheep for Thee.

Dannie Abse

F.R.S.L.

Doctor, Poet and Playwright

Paddy Ryan, well-known reprobate, embezzler, womaniser, lay on his death bed.

The priest bent over him, saying, 'Now Paddy, will yer renounce the devil an' all his evil ways?'

Paddy opened one blue eye and replied quietly, 'Ach no, fadder, this is no time to make influential enemies . . .'

Arthur R. Ashe
Tennis Player (Wimbledon Champion 1975) and Author

It seems that a very poor boy, who was brought up under very dire circumstances, was a very high achiever. He did extremely well in school and, even though his mother was an illiterate woman who never went past the sixth grade, her son did extremely well and, on his academic background, he graduated from Harvard University magna cum laude.

He then went on to graduate from Harvard Law School at the top of his class. As a gesture of appreciation to his mother for her sacrifices in getting him this far, he sent her a very rare, prized and expensive bird. After about a month or so, he 'phoned his mother to see how she was enjoying this rare and expensive gift that he had purchased for her. His mother's reply was, 'It was delicious!'

Aghast, the young man declaimed to his mother, 'Mother, that bird was exceedingly rare. It was very expensive, very bright, and it spoke five languages.'

To which his mother replied, 'Well, if it was so damn smart, why didn't it say something?'

Vladimir Ashkenazy
Concert Pianist and Conductor

A long time ago, a merchant travelled many days, weeks
and months to sell his wares. One day he arrived at the
court of a great Emperor. The Emperor liked his goods
and the trading was going well when the Emperor
noticed a large sack that was standing apart from the
others. The Emperor asked what was in it.

'Nothing special,' replied the merchant. 'It is simply
something I use in my cooking.'

'What is it called?' asked the Emperor.

'Onions, Your Majesty.'

'I have never heard of onions!'

'In that case, may I offer to cook Your Majesty a meal
with onions?' said the merchant.

When the meal was over, the Emperor exclaimed that
this was the most delicious food he had ever had and
said he would buy all the onions. 'You will not be
disappointed. I will fill your sack instead with the most
valuable treasures that I have,' said the Emperor.

And, indeed, when the merchant opened his sack on
his way home, he found in it gold, rubies, diamonds and
other precious articles, the likes of which he had never
seen before.

When he arrived home, the word spread about his
good fortune in the faraway land and another merchant
decided to try his luck. He too travelled a long time to the
same court and, during the trading with the same
Emperor, he put one sack apart. Sure enough the
Emperor asked about the contents of the sack and the
merchant said:

'Nothing special, it is something I use in my cooking.'

'What is it called?'

'Garlic, Your Majesty.'

'Garlic? I have never heard of garlic!' said the Emperor.

'In that case, may I offer to cook Your Majesty a meal with garlic?'

When this meal was over, the Emperor exclaimed that this was the most delicious food he had ever had and that he would buy all the garlic. 'You will not be disappointed. I'll fill your sack instead with the most valuable treasure that I have,' said the Emperor.

When the merchant opened his sack on the way home, he found it full of . . . onions.

A 'Musical Friend'

'Morny, rune sore-bees.'

'Oh sorry, I thought I dialled room service.'

'Rye. Rune sore-bees. Morny. Jewish to odor sunteen?'

'Yes, order something. This is Room Thirteen-Oh-Five. I want. . . .'

'Okay, torino-fie. Yes plea?'

'I'd like some bacon and eggs.'

'Ow July then?'

'What?'

'Aches. Ow July then? Fry, boy, pooch . . .?'

'Oh, the eggs! How do I like them! Sorry. Scrambled, please.'

'Ow July the baycome? Crease?'

'Crisp will be fine.'

'Okay. An Santos?'

'What?'

'Santos. July Santos?'

'Uh . . . I don't know . . . I don't think so . . .'

'No? Judo one toes?'

'Look, I really feel bad about this, but I just don't know what judo one toes means. I'm sorry.'

'Toes! Toes! Why Jew Don Juan toes? Ow bow eenlish mopping we bother?'

'English muffin! I've got it! Toast! You were saying toast! Fine. An English muffin will be fine.'

'We bother?'

'No, just put the bother on the side.'

'Wad?'

'I'm sorry, I meant butter. Butter on the side.'

'Copy?'

'I feel terrible about this, but . . .'

'Copy. Copy, tea, mill . . .'

'Coffee!! Yes, coffee please. And that's all.'

'One Minnie. Ass rune torino-fie, strangle-aches, crease baycome, tossy eenlish mopping we bother honey sigh and copy, Rye?'

'Whatever you say.'

'Okay. Tenjewberrymud.'

'You're welcome.'

Nina Bawden

M.A., F.R.S.L., J.P.
Novelist

On a journalist assignment in Florida eighteen months ago, it occurred to me that if I had been a visitor from another planet, perhaps an anthropologist from Mars, taking statistical notes on the local population, I would have concluded that the inhabitants consisted of young Hispanics who, in the course of time, underwent a curious transmogrification into elderly Americans.

Margaret A. Boden

F.B.A., M.A., Ph.D.

Research Professor of Cognitive Sciences,
University of Sussex

A self-made businessman had become so stupendously rich that he never wasted his own time in negotiating contracts, nor even in signing them. Instead, he employed an army of in-house lawyers who dealt with all such matters on his behalf.

But one day a deal was negotiated which was so daring, so ambitious, and so potentially lucrative, that the other side insisted that the boss himself attend the final meeting to sign the documents – and he agreed.

When it came to the point of signature he turned to his co-signatory and said: 'You know, of course, that I'm a self-made man, and proud of it. Why, I left school at twelve unable to read and write – and I still can't write. I've been so busy doing deals all these years that I've never had the time to learn. I can't even write my own name.'

'Amazing!' said the other, and whispered hurriedly to his own lawyer. 'However, it doesn't matter. I'm informed that it's perfectly legal, given these witnesses, for you to make your mark on the documents by putting a cross on the dotted line.'

Accepting a diamond-encrusted gold pen from his assistant, the businessman carefully wrote two crosses on the parchment.

'What have you done?'

'I've made my mark – you agreed that it's acceptable by law.'

'Yes, yes. But the *second* cross – what's that?'

'That? – Oh, that. That's my Ph.D.'

*   *   *

Of all the rivalries between the different colleges of the University of Cambridge, none is so deeply felt as that between Trinity College and Trinity Hall – both situated on the Banks of the River Cam.

Trinity is very old, beautiful, very large, very rich, very famous – and very arrogant (at a dinner to celebrate one of its Fellow's winning the Nobel Prize some years ago, the Master began his speech: 'Anywhere else, I could say that this is a very special occasion . . .').

Trinity Hall is also very old, and also very beautiful. But it is very small – and, by Trinity's standards, not rich at all. The students, and in a less adolescent way the Fellows, never fail to score a point against the other institution if they can. And the whole student body of the University may be involved: a student from another college will usually be 'for' Trinity and 'against' Trinity Hall – or (if he or she has any sense!) *vice versa*.

In a chemistry lecture one day, the lecturer (a Fellow of Pembroke) described a truly elegant and amazing chemical technique, which he remarked was 'discovered in the 1930s in this University, at Trinity.' For the next thirty seconds or so, he examined his beautifully manicured nails while the audience (consisting largely of medical students, renowned for their youthful high spirits) clapped, cheered, and stamped their feet – or booed, hissed, and jeered with equal abandon.

When the tumult had died down the lecturer looked up from his fingernails, smiled sweetly, and said: '. . . Hall.'

The Rt. Hon. Lord Boyd-Carpenter
P.C.
Politician and Author

When Winston Churchill was speaking in the House of Commons, another M.P. – a Mr. Paling – interrupted him and shouted, 'Dirty dog!'

Churchill swung round, with a beaming smile, and said, 'The Honourable Member knows what dirty dogs do to palings.'

Katie Boyle
Television Personality

I'm quite appalling at telling stories and always mis-time the pay-off line, but for its quiet humour I can tell you a gentle tale which did, in fact, happen 'after a public dinner'!

My husband, Peter Saunders, was giving his annual party to the cast of *The Mousetrap*, which happened to coincide with his birthday, and I'd had the bright (?) idea of getting a kissogram girl dressed up as a mouse for the occasion. Unfortunately, she was a little too much of an extrovert and, in front of everyone, climbed over his lap and sang 'Happy Birthday to You', then plonked a large kiss on his very embarrassed face. He was obviously not amused!

I spied his manager, Verity Hudson, and said rather worriedly, 'I think Peter is going to kill me.' As I waited for sympathetic reassurance, she looked at me coldly and said, 'Well if he doesn't, I will.'

I was then taken firmly by the hand by my furious husband and marched out before coffee was served – like a small child – in front of a flabbergasted cast!!

The Rt. Hon. The Lord Brandon of Oakbrook

M.C., P.C.

A Lord of Appeal in Ordinary

Judge A and Judge B meet at their Inn of Court. Judge A says to Judge B: 'I see from *The Times* that one of your judgments has been upheld by the Court of Appeal.'

'Yes,' replies Judge B, 'but I still think I was right.'

Gyles Brandreth
Television Personality

When I was about ten years old I was taken to the theatre to see my first 'real play' as opposed to a pantomime. I can't remember what the piece was called, but I know it was a Victorian melodrama and starred that great British actor, Sir Donald Wolfit. He played the part of a cruel and brutal father who, at the end of the play, gets his just deserts when he is stabbed to death by his own son.

Unfortunately, on the night my parents took me to see the play, at the Opera House in Manchester I think it was, the climax did not go entirely as planned. In the final moments of the drama, when Donald Wolfit was downstage ranting and raving as only he could, the young son entered, looking suitably wild-eyed and homicidal and dressed in a somewhat prematurely bloodstained greatcoat. The father, oblivious to his son's presence, went on roaring, while the tension mounted.

At last the moment for the murder was upon us. The youth crept up behind his doomed papa. With patricide clearly in mind, he plunged his hand inside his greatcoat to produce the dagger with which to perform the dreadful deed. But alas, on the night in question, dagger was there none. The distraught young man felt frantically in all his pockets, looked desperately about him and then, not knowing how else to despatch his demented father, decided to give Sir Donald a boot up the backside.

Clearly the great actor had not been expecting this surprise attack from (and to) his rear, but as he staggered towards the footlights, fell to his knees and expired, by way of simple explanation he exclaimed with his dying fall: 'That boot – that boot – 'twas poisoned!'

The Rt. Hon. Viscountess Bridgeman

M.A.

Author and Founder of the Bridgeman Art Library

Lord Nuffield, to the Oxford College porter who produced his hat for him the minute he appeared: 'How do you know it's mine, Albert?'

Albert: 'I don't, sir, but it's the one you came with.'

*　　　*　　　*

Speaker: 'I'm a little bit nervous of standing up and speaking to you tonight. You must know the story of the Hampshire vicar who made the usual parish announcement after his sermon and added "Guest speakers for the next three weeks will be nailed to the vestry door."'

Sickert, the painter, seeing a friend out, called after him when he reached the gate: 'Come again when you can't stay quite so long.'

*   *   *

Lady Astor, canvassing for her first parliamentary seat in Portsmouth, because of her status and because she was new to the town, was allotted a senior naval officer as a minder, and together they went round knocking at doors.

'Is your mother at home?' asked Lady Astor imperiously, when one door was opened by a small girl.

'No,' replied the child, 'but she said if a lady comes in with a sailor, they're to use the upstairs room and leave ten bob.'

B. J. Brown

C.B.E., F.P.
Past Sheriff of the City of London, 1977
Past Chief Commoner, 1981

I remember a Fletchers' Company dinner at Mansion House when Lord Mais was Lord Mayor. Just as the Master rose to propose the toast to the Lord Mayor, water started pouring through the ceiling of the Egyptian Hall just to the right of him. He was quite unaware of the happening which continued with increasing volume, but afterwards said he could not understand why nobody was looking at him while he made his speech, but seemed to be looking over his shoulder. Lord Mais afterwards explained that the Lady Mayoress had left the bath running.

*   *   *

Sir Robin Gillett, with whom I was Sheriff for six weeks, used to describe the ornaments in the Egyptian Hall as part of his speeches. On one occasion, having described the attractive young lady statute facing him and referred to the loss of her fingers, he spoke of another young lady statue behind him which was rather marked with dark lines which he attributed to varicose veins. However, when turning round to indicate the young lady statue he found to his consternation a young lady interpreter standing there.

*   *   *

Lord Donaldson is reported as making the shortest speech ever at a reception hosted by him and his wife:
   'I plead not guilty, but enter a plea for mitigation through my mouthpiece,' and he handed over to his wife.

Helen Gurley Brown

Author, and Editor-in-Chief, Cosmopolitan Magazine
International Edition

Two pirates run into each other and after the initial greeting, one says to the other, 'My God, Angus, what happened to *you*?'

'I guess you're talking about my pegged leg.'

'I certainly am.'

'Well, the other day I was out on the rigging and fell into the water. Before I could get back on the ship's deck a shark got me and now I've got the peg.'

'What happened to your arm?'

'Oh, you're referring to the hook. Well, I ran into a young swashbuckler recently and you know how it is. We started to fight and since I'm not swashing and buckling as well as I once did, he got my right arm. Now it's the hook.'

'And what about your eye?'

'You're referring to the patch over my eye? I was up in the crow's nest and a pigeon dropped on my eye and put it out.'

'So, I can understand your losing your leg to the sharks and possibly your right arm in a duel with a younger man, but I cannot see why the droppings of the pigeon would cause you to lose the sight of your eye.'

'It can if that's your first day with the hook!'

General Sir Edward Burgess
K.C.B., O.B.E.
National President of the Royal British Legion

The Penalty of Smugness

Three candidates for Heaven are queuing at St. Peter's Gate. St. Peter, casting a jaundiced eye on the first applicant, asks: 'Have you always been faithful to your wife?' The answer comes unctuously in the affirmative. 'Right,' says St. Peter, 'you can have a white Rolls-Royce to drive around Heaven.'

Turning to the second, St. Peter poses the same question. The second, looking shifty, replies: 'Well, more or less; there have been lapses.'

'Right,' says St. Peter, 'you can have a white Ford to drive around Heaven.'

Finally, he turns to the third man, who says: 'Before you ask me, I have taken my fun where I found it and nobody could describe me as faithful.'

'Right,' says St. Peter, 'you can have a white Mini.'

Driving his white Mini around a cloud the third man spots the Rolls-Royce parked beside the cloud with the driver in tears. 'What is wrong with you?' he says. 'You've got nothing to be miserable about, you've got the best car in Heaven.'

'I know,' says the driver of the Rolls-Royce, 'but I've just seen my wife go past on a white skateboard.'

The Rt. Hon. Lord Carr of Hadley

P.C.

Politician and Author
Past Leader of the House of Commons
Past Home Secretary

Essay by an eight-year-old boy about Grandmothers, quoted by the (then) Archbishop of Canterbury (Dr. Donald Coggan) in a House of Lords debate on 'The Family in Britain Today' on 16 June 1976

'A grandmother is a lady who has no children of her own, so she likes other people's little girls and boys. A grandfather is a man grandmother. He goes for walks with the boys and they talk about fishing and tractors. Grandmothers don't have to do anythng but be there. They are old, so they shouldn't play hard or run. They should never say, "Hurry up." Usually they are fat, but not too fat to tie children's shoes. They wear glasses and funny underwear and they can take their teeth and gums off. They don't have to be smart, only answer questions like why dogs hate cats and why God isn't married. They don't talk baby-talk, like visitors. When they read to us, they don't skip bits, or mind if it is the same story over again. Everybody should have one, especially if you don't have television, because grandmothers are the only grown-ups who have time.'

*   *   *

The Self-Important Politician

A particularly self-important politician went to a grand reception one evening without his invitation. He thought this would not matter because obviously he would be well known. But at the door he encountered a commissionaire who had other ideas – an imposing figure of a man in equally imposing uniform. Much to the

M.P.'s chagrin, the commissionaire insisted that he wait in the hall while enquiries were made.

'But don't you know who I am?' said the M.P. indignantly, drawing himself up to his full but rather limited height.

'No, sir,' said the commissionaire, 'but I will go and find out and let you know!'

*   *   *

A Moral Tale for Politicians Too Anxious to Please

A peasant took his son with his one donkey on a journey to see the boy's grandparents.

On the first day, the father rode and the son walked. 'How cruel to the child,' was the comment in the village where they stopped for the night.

On the second day, the father walked and the son rode. But the comments of the villagers that night were, 'What has the young generation come to?'

On the third day, they both rode on the donkey only to be met at night by the complaint of cruelty to animals.

So on the fourth day, the father made them both walk and left the donkey unladen. 'Oh,' said the villagers that night, 'they must be mad. Lock them up!'

The Rt. Hon. Lord Carrington

K.C.M.G., M.C., P.C.

Secretary General of NATO, 1984–88

Years ago, when I was High Commissioner in Australia, I was given a Civic Reception in a town in the West.

Waiting at the bottom end of the Town Hall to go on to the platform to make a speech, I was a little surprised when, at a signal from the Mayor, the audience stood up and sang as we processed up the aisle:

'SEE THE MIGHTY HOST ADVANCING
SATAN LEADING ON.'

Sir Hugh Casson

C.H., K.C.V.O., P.P.R.A., R.D.I.

Architect and Author, Past President of the Royal
Academy

When Charles II visited St. John's College, Oxford, he
was shown a portrait of Charles I. He asked whether he
could have it. The College demurred.

'I will grant you any favour in return,' said Charles II.

'In that case,' said the College, 'of course, it is yours.'

'Thank you,' said the King; and 'What now is your
request?'

'Give it back, please,' they said.

(He did, and the portrait is still in the College library.)

*　　　*　　　*

Overheard coming up the staircase at Burlington House:
'He's French, but she's terribly nice!'

Alderman John Chalstrey

M.D., F.R.C.S.

Consultant Surgeon

A High Court judge enters his court and finds that there are three barristers waiting.

The first arises and says, 'M'lud, I appear for the prosecution.'

The second also stands and says, 'M'lud, I appear for the defence.'

With considerable dignity, the third barrister arises and says, 'M'lud, I appear to be in the wrong court!'

His Excellency Mr. Ji Chaozho
Past Ambassador of the People's Republic of China

An old man had a bedroom just above his own to let. As he was particularly sensitive to all sorts of noise, it was quite some time before he found an unsociable young tenant.

The young man happened to be a policeman, who wore very heavy boots. On the first night he moved in, he dropped his boots without much thought while going to bed. The old man made a complaint on the following morning, saying he had heart trouble and would really appreciate it if his tenant could be more careful with his boots. The young man apologised with all sincerity.

The policeman came home exhausted that evening. After letting fall the first boot, he suddenly remembered what he was told that morning. Feeling guilty, he very gently laid down on the floor the second boot.

Early next morning, an angry knocking at the door awoke the poor man and he opened the door to his irritated landlord. 'What on earth was wrong with you?' exclaimed the old man. 'I was terrified by the first boot and waited the whole night for the second!'

The Rt. Hon. Lord Charteris of Amisfield

G.C.B., K.C.B., G.C.V.O., P.C.

Provost of Eton since 1978

Computers when programmed to translate from one language to another are unreliable. For example, the phrase in English:

'The Spirit is willing but the flesh is weak!'
comes out in Russian as:

'The Vodka is fine but the meat is awful!'

The Rt. Hon. Lord Cledwyn of Penrhos

C.H., P.L.

Past Leader of the Opposition, House of Lords

A famous Welsh rugby player passed away and found himself at the Pearly Gates. He gave his name to the Saint who asked him if he had any confessions to make. He admitted that he had several, such as the time he scored a try in an international match against England when in fact he had committed a foul which the referee did not see. He went on to cite a number of similar cases for which he said he was extremely contrite.

Eventually the Saint said, 'Very well Jenkins, you have made your confession, you can now come in.' Jenkins said, 'Oh, thank you very much St. Peter,' whereupon the Saint said, 'Oh, I am not St. Peter, he is on leave. I am St. David.'

Sir Colin Cole

K.C.V.O., M.V.O., T.D., F.S.A.

Past Garter Principal King of Arms, 1978–1992
Author of Articles on Heraldry

On the occasion of Queen Victoria's Golden Jubilee, in 1887, it was proposed that the statue of Queen Anne, which stood outside St. Paul's, should be moved.

Queen Victoria is reported to have said: 'Move Queen Anne? Most certainly not! Why, it might some day be suggested that *my* statue should be moved, which I should much dislike.'

Lady Georgina Coleridge
Author and Journalist

My Aunt!!

My Great Aunt Christine's absent-mindedness was a family legend. She was said to have failed to recognise her own youngest son at a children's party, and to have tipped a taxi driver with her return ticket to Scotland. The many stories (some not quite as true as this one) started at the end of World War One.

Her son John had been ordered to the South of France to recover from war wounds. So, determined to escort him, she crossed the Channel in a whirl, surrounded by a mountain of luggage. (There were plenty of porters then.) And there were parcels, rugs, books, baskets, handbags and hatboxes . . . Poor John dreaded travelling with his mother, who always fidgeted constantly, moving bits of luggage about and losing gloves, scarves or handkerchiefs every few minutes.

At last they settled down in a reserved carriage, and John slept, exhausted, for about twenty minutes. Then there was a fearful screech of brakes and a cloud of steam as the Express shuddered to a halt.

Christine had hooked her umbrella to the communication cord.

John paid the fine and apologised profusely – and the train started again after a long delay, during which Christine sat in silent amazement.

They had been going another half hour or so when she prodded John awake. 'Darling,' she said plaintively, 'I still cannot understand why those men made such a fuss. All I did was this . . .' – and she hooked her umbrella firmly back on to the communication cord.

They spend that night in a police station.

Sir Kenneth Cork

C.B.E., D.Litt., F.C.A.

Lord Mayor of London, 1978–79

There were two bankrupts, one rich and one poor. Both wanted money to save their businesses. They knew it was no use going to the banks, for they only lend you money when you don't want it. So the only thing to do was to go to the Church and pray.

The rich man, as was his right, went to the front of the Church and prayed. 'God,' he said, 'my business is broke and I need a million pounds. As You know, it is no use going to the banks, but You have all the money in the world. You have all the gold in Fort Knox; all the oil in the desert; all the treasures of the world. So You would not miss a million pounds.'

The poor bankrupt also prayed to God. 'Lord, my business is in trouble and all I need is five hundred pounds. You have all the money in the world and You would not miss five hundred pounds.'

At this, the rich bankrupt got up, went to the poor bankrupt and said, 'The Lord has heard your prayer. Here is my cheque for five hundred pounds, drawn on a Swiss bank, so it will be met. Go away, and rejoice and thank the Lord.'

The poor man left the Church, praising the Lord, and the rich bankrupt went back on his knees, saying, 'Now, Lord, can I have your undivided attention?'

*　　*　　*

There was a single-handed sailor sailing off the Isle of Wight. It was very rough, and the boat began to sink. A larger liner saw what was happening, turned towards the yacht and came alongside.

'Come aboard,' shouted the skipper, 'you are going to drown.'

'I do not need any help – go away. I have absolute faith in my God and my boat,' was the reply.

So, much annoyed, the liner turned back on its course.

It was one of those rare days when the Coastguards happened to be looking out to sea, and so alarmed were they that they called out the lifeboat. The lifeboat forced its way through mountainous seas and came alongside the sinking yacht.

'Come aboard,' they shouted, 'you are going to drown.'

'Go away,' the skipper replied. 'I have absolute faith in my God and my boat.'

It got rougher and the yacht sunk further. The Coastguards called out a naval chopper. They let down a crewman on his bit of rope, and he called to the skipper: 'Let us winch you aboard or you will drown.'

'Go away! I have absolute faith in my God and my ship. I do not need any help.'

So, somewhat annoyed, the chopper went away.

The inevitable happened, and the sailor drowned. Being a godly man, he went to heaven and was met by God at the Pearly Gates.

'I am very disappointed in you, God,' said he. 'I have absolute faith in you, and yet here I am – drowned.'

'I am disappointed too,' said God. I sent you a liner; I sent you a lifeboat; I sent you a chopper – and you still managed to get drowned.'

M. Colin Cowdrey

Cricketer (Past England Captain, twenty-three times) and Author

'Kipper' Cowdrey

My nickname is 'The Kipper' – for I used to have the knack of being able to shut my eyes for a ten minute nap, or a 'kip', at will, whether in the car, the train or the airport waiting for the flight to be called.

It all began during my first Test Match at Adelaide, with the temperature steaming in the hundreds. I came off for lunch soaking wet, pulled off my clothes, showered, took a cold drink and lay under a towel in the bench in the dressing room fast asleep. The ground was packed, some 40,000 people, and the match tense and poised, my batting partner Denis Compton.

Five minutes before the umpires went out I was woken up by the twelfth man, Vic Wilson, a delightful Yorkshireman. He helped me on with my clothes. Relaxed and refreshed, Denis Compton and I enjoyed a hundred partnership during the afternoon. My colleagues could not get over it and named me 'Kipper of the Year'!

In the next Test Match, for some reason, the ability to sleep seemed to desert me. The dressing room seemed very noisy and I could not make myself comfortable. An hour later, I walked to the wicket and was out first ball!

I was accused of not concentrating – on sleep at lunch time, or before going to the crease. I had really started something. I never lost the tag as 'The Kipper' supreme.

Wendy Craig

(in collaboration with her husband, Jack Bentley)
Actress

Two little boys were talking.

'Do you know what I found in Daddy's bureau this morning?'

'No,' replied his brother.

'A packet of contraceptives.'

'Oooh,' his brother's eyes widened. 'What's a bureau?'

The Rt. Hon. The Lord Cudlipp

O.B.E.

Author

I always thought penicillin was discovered and
christened by Sir Alexander Fleming in 1929. And that its
medical uses were developed at the start of the Hitler
War. And that the lion's share of the credit went to Sir
Howard Florey and his team of Oxford researchers who
were investigating antibiotics.

That's what I used to think and that's what the
reference books, medical and otherwise, are still saying.
But now I'm not so sure. If we ever meet up in an airport
bar on a foggy night, I'd like to know what you think of
the story I heard when I was held up by a tropical storm
at the airport in Darwin, Australia.

The talking came from a local medical sergeant over a
long, cool beer. He pointed to the hospital hutments a
hundred yards away . . .

'We picked up this abo – I am in the Flying Medical
Corps – in a village 150 miles from here. He had been
bitten by a crocodile, a big, ugly bastard, and the teeth
had lacerated him right across his chest and back.

'To say that the wounds were septic is putting it
mildly.

'The doctor I was with said, "This abo's had it, but
we'll fly him to Darwin and see." We cauterised the
wounds, stitched him up and waited for him to join his
ancestors.

'I'm on my hospital rounds a week later and find that
this abo has vanished, vamoosed; there was positively no
abo in that bed, you can take my word for that. So we
forget about the abo until the doc and I fly to the same
village one month later. He had done his best, the doc
told the chief. And then the chief took us for a walk in
the bush – and there was that same abo laughing his
bloody head off. Search me, I can't explain it, I'm only
telling you what happened. The little runt had woken

44

up, felt lonely, and headed south – just like a homing pigeon.

'All the stitches had burst open in the bush, and God knows how and what he ate, or how he found his way. All we could get out of the chief – he was a little runt too – was that his cobbers in the tribe had filled his bleeding wounds with mud from the river where the crocodile had got him.'

What did I make of that, asked the medical sergeant. Well, what do you make of it? Alexander Fleming produced penicillin from a mould or fungi that flourished in a damp atmosphere . . . maybe like the river-bed in the Northern Territory of Australia where the croc half gobbled up the abo. But I don't recollect any aborigine's name appearing in the New Year's Honours List, do you?

The Rt. Hon. Baron Delfont of Stepney
Impressario

Many years ago, as a young and struggling impressario, I
invested what truly was the last of my miniscule
resources in a production of *Goodnight Vienna* at
Wandsworth Town Hall.

Fearing not only for my peace of mind, but also for my
physical safety, which I was certain would be at risk from
a doubtless less-than-satisfied audience, I did not attend
the 'opening night'. It was, in fact, a full four days before
I plucked up the courage to pay the 'show' a visit!

Motor transport being beyond my meagre means, I
was left to suffer the wiles of British Railways.
Consequently I did not arrive until well after curtain-up.

I proceeded through the stage door, to be met by the
elderly 'keeper'.

'Yes?' he grunted.

'Good evening,' I said, in my best East London accent.
'I'm Bernard Delfont, and this is my show. I just dropped
in to see how *Goodnight Vienna* was doing in
Wandsworth.'

'It's doing about as well,' he replied, 'as *Goodnight
Wandsworth* would do in Vienna!'

The Rt. Hon. Viscount de L'Isle

V.C., K.G., P.C., G.C.N.G., G.C.V.O.

Past President of the Freedom Association, Chairman of
Trustees, Churchill Memorial Trust

The shortest and saddest school report:
  'He does his best, I'm afraid!'

The Rt. Hon. Lord Denham

P.C.

Government Chief Whip, House of Lords
Author

A man out hunting, perfectly dressed in scarlet coat and
top hat, was sitting on his horse by the covertside,
watching two girls also on horses struggling
unsuccessfully to open a gate. A man in gumboots,
obviously a local farmer, came stumping by.

'I say,' said the man on the horse, 'you see those two
girls? They're not having much success – would you be
very kind and go and give them a hand?'

'That's all very well,' said the farmer, 'but you *are* on
the horse and it's a very muddy field. Why don't you do
it?'

'Well, it's a bit embarrassing, really. One of them's my
wife and the other's my mistress and I don't want them
to see me together.'

The farmer's face cleared. 'I quite understand,' he said.
'I'm a man of the world myself. Of course I'll do it,' and
he went stumping off across the plough.

Halfway there, he turned abruptly and, much to the
other's surprise, came stumping rather more quickly back
again. As he drew level with the horseman, he paused
and looked up at him.

'By God, it's a small world,' he said.

Kirk Douglas
Actor

I grew up in Amsterdam, New York, a mill town in the Mohawk River Valley where my parents settled after migrating from Russia. On our street was every conceivable nationality, a little League of Nations: Italian, Polish, Irish, Russian, German, British, Lithuanian and many others. They had names like Stosh, Ginga and Yabo. That was *after* they were Americanised.

I always liked 'Wolfie', real name Wilfred Churchett, who had come to America with his family from England. Wolfie was three or four years older than I, big, but with a gentleness about him that was soothing after the rough-house gang on my street. I often sat on his front stoop playing a game of baseball that he had created. It was a cut-out, a piece of cardboard, with different sections marked 'Base on Balls', 'Sacrifice Bunt', 'Two-Base Hit', 'Trickle to Pitcher', 'Outfield Error', etc. Then he would put in an arrow and spin it round. Since there were seven kids in our house and my mother and father made nine, he would make my whole family a baseball team and get each one up to bat and spin around and see what happened. I was delighted when my mother got up to bat and hit a home run.

When I was eight, they were building another mill near my house. A huge, deep trench was dug for the foundation. A pipe broke, filling it with water. One Saturday, wearing my best clothes – my only suit – I tried to walk across the trench on a pole, slipped and fell in. The other kids ran away, frightened. The water was well over my head. I was drowning, the water closing in over me. Suddenly, there was Wolfie rushing towards me. He pulled me out, brought me home crying and soaking wet – but *alive*.

The Rt. Hon. Sir Edward du Cann
P.C., K.B.E.
Politician and Author

There was a businessman who sought to buy a brassiere for his wife.

'I want a size thirteen and three-quarters,' he told the assistant.

The assistant patiently explained that a more usual size would be thirty-six inches, but the businessman insisted that thirteen and three-quarters was the correct measure.

'How do you arrive at this figure?' he was asked.

'My head size is six and seven-eighths, so thirteen and three-quarters corresponds to two bowler hats.'

The Very Reverend R.M.S. Eyre
Dean of Exeter

Provost Phelps, besides being a very great and famous talker, was also a stickler for etiquette, particularly in the Common Room after dinner in Hall. He particularly insisted that the port and decanters should never be lifted, but always slid from person to person in their coasters. On one occasion, a Colonial Bishop was dining and, not knowing the Oriel habits, he lifted the port decanter to pass it to his neighbour, who was the Provost.

At that, Phelps burst out with a cry of: 'Slide it, man, slide it!'

Everyone was rather embarrassed at this outburst and did their best to cover it up. A little later on, strawberries were produced in silver dishes. With a suave expression, the Bishop turned to the Provost and said:

'Provost, may I slide you some strawberries?'

It was the only recorded occasion on which Provost Phelps was reduced to silence.

The Lord Fanshaw

K.C.M.G.

President of the Assembly of Council of Europe and
W.E.U.
Past Under-Secretary of State for Foreign and
Commonwealth Affairs

A young man was asked by his housemaster at school if
he was troubled by sexual thoughts.

He answered: 'Oh no, I enjoy them enormously.'

*   *   *

General Eisenhower arrived in London during the war
and visited Soho for the first time. Pavements were
blocked with Ladies of the Street.

'What is this?' he asked. 'A jam of tarts?'

His English, and well-educated, A.D.C. replied: 'No,
sir. A volume of Trollope's or a line of English pro's.'

*   *   *

Irate voter to Parliamentary candidate: 'What? You want
me to vote for you? I would not vote for you if you were
the Archangel Gabriel.'

The candidate replied: 'If I were the Archangel Gabriel,
you would not be in my constituency.'

*   *   *

Boring speakers remind me of the famous old politician
who, having talked interminably and boringly about
himself, turned to his companion and said, 'I have talked
about myself long enough. Let's talk about you. What do
you think of me?'

Bryan Forbes
Actor, Producer, Director and Author

There was a male fashion model who lived in an apartment block in New York, whose two passions in life were his cat and his mother. One day he got a call from his agent with the offer of a lucrative job in Los Angeles which he dearly wanted to accept, but he could not bear to leave his cat. So he approached his downstairs neighbour and asked if he would look after the animal during his absence.

'I'll leave all his food and I'll ring every night from L.A. to make sure he's all right.'

His neighbour accepted the chore and the model departed for sunny California. True to his word, he rang on the first night to enquire after his pet. Everything was fine. The cat wasn't fretting, had eaten his food and used the cat tray.

The second night he rang again and his neighbour said, 'I'm sorry, your cat died.' The model was so shocked, he collapsed and hung up.

He rang the following night and said, 'I simply don't understand how you could be so callous.'

The neighbour replied, 'Well, I'm sorry, obviously I was insensitive, but the cat was dead and I just blurted it out – what else could I have said?'

'Well,' the model replied, 'you could have broken it to me gently. You could have said, "Listen, don't worry, but your cat is on the roof. I've sent for the Fire Brigade and everything's going to be fine." Then the next night when I rang, you could have said, "We did all we could, but sadly the experience proved too much for your cat and he passed away peacefully." In that way, I would have been prepared and I could have handled it.'

'Okay, you're right,' his neighbour said. 'I guess I don't have much finesse. I apologise.'

'I have recovered a bit now, that's why I can just about accept it,' the model said. 'Anyway, since I'm on the 'phone, has my mother been in touch?'

There was a long pause, then his neighbour said: 'Well . . . as it happens, your mother is on the roof . . .'

Sir Vivian Fuchs

M.A., Ph.D., F.R.S.
Explorer and Author

Why is a Ship called 'She'?

Because there is always a great deal of bustle around her; there is usually a gang of men about; it takes a lot of paint to keep her good-looking; it is not the initial expense that breaks you – it is the upkeep; she can be all decked out; it takes an experienced man to handle her correctly; and without a man in charge she is absolutely uncontrollable.

She shows her topsides, hides her bottom and, when coming into port, always heads for the buoys.

G. W. H. Gibbs

F.R.S.A., M.I.P.A.
Publicist

As a member of a parents' association, I visited a local school and was granted the privilege of sitting in on the morning lessons of a class of eleven-year-olds.

The first lesson was on the virtues of life, with the teacher emphasising that the most salient was telling the truth.

This was followed by a lesson on ancient history, at the end of which the teacher asked questions, one of them addressed to Smith minor:

'Tell me, Smith minor, what do you know about the ancient Britons?'

Smith minor replied: 'Sir, if I follow the precept of the previous lesson, then in truth my answer must be that my knowledge of ancient Britons is absolutely nothing.'

*   *   *

The best after dinner speech I have ever heard is:
'I'll take the bill!'

*   *   *

At a medical officers' luncheon, a doctor was telling his audience of his visits to an old people's home. Of one inmate he asked how he felt about life now that he was seventy-five years old.

Unhesitatingly, the answer came: 'I prefer it to the alternative!'

*   *   *

Opening of a speech:

'Just at the moment I feel a bit like Mark Antony when he entered Cleopatra's boudoir and said: "Cleo, I came not to speak . . ." or something like that!'

Sir John Gielgud

C.H., Kt.

Actor, Producer, Director and Author

Dame Marie Tempest was a distinguished and brilliant comedienne and also something of a martinet. During the war, she was a guest at the country home of another actress and arrived accompanied by her Scottie, to whom she was devoted and had christened Fanny.

The hostess had opened an American parcel in her honour and a magnificent peach-fed ham was served at dinner. Dame Marie Tempest was in the place of honour, with her pet lying on a clean, white coverlet. Dame Marie suddenly rapped her knife on the wine glass beside her and announced, in ringing tones, 'Ham! Adrienne, this is no use to Fanny.'

*　　*　　*

Many years ago, I happened to make the acquaintance of Lady Frances Balfour, the mother of a friend of mine. She was a famous feminist, very strict and Victorian, wearing Mary, Queen of Scots, bonnets and disapproving of the theatre, though most charmingly polite to me because of my friendship with her son.

Jean Cadell, a brilliant actress, happened to be a kinswoman of Lady Frances, and so was also tolerated by her. It was she who told me this story, which occurred when Miss Cadell was invited to lunch.

As they sat over their cottage pie and blancmange, the maid entered with a large parcel wrapped in paper.

'What have you got there?' asked Lady Frances.

To which the maid replied, 'It's from Her Royal Highness, Princess Louise, your Ladyship, and she wants the box back.'

Rumer Godden
Writer, Playwright and Poet

We authors are usually the most conceited of people (though, of course, we pretend not to be) with a great addiction to the pronoun 'I'.

My literary agent, the late Spencer Curtis Brown, and his wife, Jean, used to play a game when they had to go to any dinner party which included an author.

This was in the days when small dishes of salted almonds were often put along the table, I suppose to be nibbled at between courses. The game was that Spencer and Jean would take it in turns to introduce a topic as far away from that particular author's experience as they could get – say, a name for the newest planet; were crocodiles truthfully man-eaters? who would succeed to the Kingdom on the death of the Wali of Swot? They would then see if the author would, within three sentences, contrive to bring the conversation back to himself/herself. It usually only took two.

Husband or wife would then put the requisite number of salted almonds in front of their plates. The fewest number of almonds won.

Sir Arthur Gold

Kt., C.B.E.

Past President of the European Atheletic Association,
Chairman of the Commonwealth Games Council for
England

During a cheerful diplomatic party, the British and Soviet
Ambassadors were discussing their past athletic prowess.

To compare their current form they strolled out to the
sidewalk, paced out 100 yards and proceeded to run a
two-man race – which the Brit. won.

The next morning, the sports page of *Pravda* duly
carried the following report:

'In Washington last night the British and Soviet
Ambassadors competed in a race for diplomats. The
Soviet Ambassador finished second and the British
Ambassador one from last.'

Lord Grade
Past President ATV Network Ltd
Author

When a little girl asked me what two and two make, I replied:
  'It depends if you're buying or selling.'

Beryl Grey
C.B.E.
Prima Ballerina and Author

A little girl (before the 1939–45 war) running to school because she is late, muttering a little prayer every so often – 'Please God, don't let me be late,' and again, 'Please God, don't let me be late,' and yet again, when she trips and falls!
  Getting up hurriedly before rushing off again, she is overheard saying: 'Christ – please don't push.'

James Herriot

O.B.E., F.K.C.V.S.

Writer and Practising Veterinary Surgeon

A farmer, whose income tax affairs were in a turmoil and who was suspected of doing a bit of evasion, was told to present himself at the Inland Revenue office with his business records. After examination of the records, he was asked to pay an amount to settle his back tax.

He carefully counted out the money in cash and, when the Inspector asked him if he wanted a receipt, he looked startled.

'You're not going to put that through the books, are you?' he exclaimed.

The Rt. Hon. Lord Holderness

P.C., D.L.

Politician, President, Queen Elizabeth's Foundation for
the Disabled

A learned Professor of Literature offered his services to
lecture on the poet Keats to a Regiment, whilst he was in
the area where they were stationed. The Commanding
Officer explained that there was an Officers' Mess dinner
that night, but that the RSM was delighted with the idea,
if the Professor would be happy to lecture to the NCOs
and men. The Professor agreed; and the RSM thus
introduced him:

'We are very fortunate to have Professor Lightfoot to
come and talk to us about keats. It'll do you a lot of good.
I don't suppose any of you hignorant blighters even
know what a keat is.'

Lady Holland-Martin

D.B.E, D.L.

Chairman, National Society for the Prevention of Cruelty to Children

A small girl noticed her mother was getting rather large. Her mother, realising this, said: 'Darling, daddy has given me a little baby.'

The child was not convinced, so went to her father for confirmation.

'Yes, it is true,' he said.

'Well Daddy,' said his daughter, 'Mummy has eaten it.'

The Rt. Hon. Sir Geoffrey Howe

P.C., Kt., Q.C.

Past Secretary of State for Foreign and Commonwealth Affairs

Three Foreign Diplomats talking about family matters:
   First: 'My wife cannot have children, she is inconceivable.'
   Second: 'Don't you mean she is unbearable?'
   Third: 'No, no, you mean she is impregnable.'

Gloria Hunniford
Radio and Television Personality

A very good friend of mine makes a habit of having a
notebook at the ready and logs every interesting
comment, story or joke which he hears at various
dinners. He systematically files them under subject
headings, which means he can tailor any of his stories to
any kind of subject, and it is so interesting how a lot of
those comments which one overhears can be adapted to
personal needs. One good opener I heard goes as
follows:

'Tonight I feel like Elizabeth Taylor's sixth husband. I
know exactly *what* I should be doing, but I'm damned if I
know how to make it different!'

Sir Leonard Hutton

Kt.

Professional Cricketer and Author

In 1937, I played in my first Test Match against New Zealand at Lords.

On the Saturday, in England's first innings, I made nought. On the Sunday, which was a rest day in those days, I went to the cinema to forget about my dreadful start in Test cricket.

The newsreel came on and showed me being bowled out for a duck. Shortly afterwards, the lights went up. Two boys, sitting close by, recognised me and asked me to sign an autograph for them. This I did, but they would keep talking about the test match, so I had to depart to find some comfort elsewhere.

Better days were to follow, thank goodness.

Jeremy Irons
Actor

Recently, a small aircraft was flying over the Nevada Desert carrying three passengers: the President of the United States, a priest and a Californian hippy. Engine trouble occurred and the pilot came back into the cabin to break the news to the passengers.

'You are going to have to jump,' he told them, 'and, unfortunately, we only have two parachutes for the three of you, so you must decide amongst yourselves who is left behind.'

The President made a strong case about how he was a possible Saviour of the world, the man who single-handed is fighting Communism on all fronts and the man who is the figure-head of the free world. There was, therefore, no doubt that he should be allowed to live. The priest and the hippy agreed and, with that, the President strapped on a backpack and jumped out of the aeroplane.

Next, the priest began to say how, since he was an old man and had little more to give to the world, the last remaining parachute should be taken by the hippy. But the hippy disagreed, saying:

'Don't worry, man, there are still two parachutes, the Saviour of the world just jumped out wearing my rucksack!'

Elizabeth Jenkins

O.B.E.
Writer

A patient, whose regular doctor was away, went to his locum. The latter gave him a thorough overhaul, then said, 'There's nothing the matter with you, except that you're seriously run down. Can you take a holiday?'

The patient said, 'I suppose I can.'

'Well, do,' the doctor said. 'Take it easy and enjoy yourself. Are you fond of the theatre?'

The patient said, 'Yes, very.'

The doctor said, 'I advise you to give yourself a good laugh; go and see this new show of George Grossmith's.'

The patient said, 'But I *am* George Grossmith.'

*   *   *

Two army chaplains in the last war, a Catholic and an Anglican, had been excellent friends. When they were demobbed, the Catholic said:

'Well, my dear fellow, now we go our separate paths, you serving God in your way, and I in His.'

*   *   *

A Victorian judge said that people giving evidence came in three grades: the liar, the damned liar and the first-rate witness.

Howel Jones

Doctor
Hon. Medical Adviser to the Commonwealth Games
Federation

The game between the visiting All Blacks side and the
South Wales side had been vigorous and, finally, play
had to be stopped when a New Zealander incurred a
facial injury which left him with blood pouring out of his
mouth and staining the front of his jersey.

The silence all round the ground which had developed
as he was led off, still bleeding, was broken by the voice
of a spectator:

'Count the players, Ref – I think he has eaten one of
them!'

*   *   *

The testing of new drugs involves trials of their
effectiveness and side effects and, in order to avoid bias,
these are usually done on a double-blind basis. This
means that neither the patient nor the doctor following
up the patient knows whether the active drug or an
identical-looking placebo is being given.

A visiting American doctor who had joined our
department, which was very active in the field of drug
trials, said that in their unit in the United States they had
moved ahead from double-blind trials and they now did
triple-blind trials: the patients did not know what they
were taking, the nurse did not know what she was giving
and the doctor did not know what he was doing!

Sir John Junor

Past Editor, Sunday Express
Author

The late Duke of Norfolk, as a Jockey Club steward, was not only mad keen on racing, he was also one of the leading campaigners against stimulant drugs being given to race horses.

At dawn one morning on the day of a big race meeting, he chanced to visit his racing stables to take a look at one of his horses which was running in the big race that day. To his surprise, he discovered the trainer in the stable in the act of putting something in the horse's mouth.

'What are you doing?' cried the Duke.

The trainer sprang back in surprise. 'Nothing, your Grace. Just giving the horse a glucose sweet.' And, in so saying, he took two wrapped sweets from his pocket and offered one to the Duke. The Duke, his suspicions disarmed, unwrapped it and sucked it in his mouth. The trainer did the same with the second sweet.

Before the big race that day, the trainer was giving his instructions to the jockey on the Duke's horse. They were as follows:

He said, 'Hold her back until the six furlong mark, then let her go. If anything passes you after that, it will be either me or the Duke of Norfolk.'

The Rt. Hon. Lord Justice Kerr

P.C.

A Lord Justice of Appeal
President of the Institute of Arbitrators

Schoolmasters can be pompous, but small boys are not so easily impressed.

A mathematics master says to his class: 'You have all read the Greek legends in Homer's *Odyssey*, and you will all remember how the giant Polyphemus hurled rocks at the boat when Ulysses and his companions escaped from the cave after putting out his eye. Why do you think he missed?'

A long silence. He then says: 'Have none of you boys ever heard of parallax? Once you understand this, it is easy to see why. Close your right eye, hold your left index finger about a foot from your nose and try to touch the tip with your right index finger. You see, you all miss because it is so difficult to judge the distance with one eye, and this is all to do with parallax.'

Another silence, whereupon a boy puts up his hand and says: 'But sir, surely Polyphemus only had one eye in the middle of his forehead.'

Then a very long silence indeed before the teacher says, crossly: 'Well, that is yet another factor to be taken into consideration.'

The Lord Killearn
Major, The Scots Guards

A good speech is like a good dress – short enough to be interesting, but long enough to cover the subject.

*　　*　　*

Dowager Duchess (pre 1914): 'Winston, I don't like your politics, but I deplore your moustache.'
Winston Churchill: 'Dear Duchess, there is no reason why you should have any contact with either.'

Dame Jill Knight
D.B.E., M.P.
Politician

An elderly man was attacked in a city subway. He lay unconscious on the pavement, his spectacles smashed and blood coming from his head. A man on the opposite side glanced across but continued walking. A man on the same side came along, glanced over the poor man, walked round him and continued on his way.

Then a social worker saw the prone figure and rushed across. She knelt beside him, gazing at the gory mess.

'Whoever did *this* needs help,' she said.

Sir Larry Lamb

Kt.

Journalist

Some years ago, when I was Editor of the *Daily Express*, I suffered a massive heart attack in the office. I was snatched from the jaws of death – at Bart's, where else? – by the distinguished Gareth Rees ('Gareth the Knife') in an operation which lasted nine hours.

Private Eye later quoted an anonymous member of my staff as saying that it had taken Gareth eight hours to find my heart!

John le Carré
Writer

There was once a great conductor of music who combined most of the English virtues. He was plausible in all things, but particularly in his music. He was fluent and persuasive and never at a loss for a note. He boasted a fluent and persuasive acquaintance with many highly placed people, for whom he didn't give a damn. He rose fast and surely to the summit of his profession.

One day, this great conductor held a great concert. At the Albert Hall. All the world came. The crowned heads of Europe came. The crowned heads of industry and the sciences.

Also, his friend came. The great conductor's oldest, dearest friend, whom he had acquired only a few weeks before and had promptly appointed to be his latest Boswell.

'Old friend,' said the conductor, 'I want you to come to my dressing room in the interval and I want you to meet somebody I admire nearly as much as I admire you, who has stood by me in bad times as well as in good.'

The interval arrived. His friend prised himself free of the ecstatic audience and gained the sanctuary of the great conductor's dressing room.

And there he stood, with his back to the door, facing a long mirror, plucking at his white tie. A dresser was helping him into a fresh tail coat. A barber was tending his hair.

In a corner of the dressing room, on a sofa, sat an old, old gentleman leaning heavily on a stick. His hands were gnarled. His ancient head was bowed upon his chest. I don't know his age exactly, and I don't think he did either.

'Dear friend,' said the great conductor, smiling past his own image in the mirror as he continued to work needlessly on his immaculate appearance. 'How good of you to come. You enjoyed the music?'

'Very much.'

'I took enough bows?'

'Quite enough.'

'Allow me to present, then,' said the great conductor, 'an old and valued friend who has stood by me in bad times as well as in good.' Here a little tug at the white tie. 'His Majesty, the King of Norway.'

In awe, the conductor's friend turned to the old, old man in the corner and, like the great conductor himself, he too bowed, though only once.

But as he bowed, the old man began shaking his head. First gently, as if waking. Then vigorously, as if contradicting. Finally he spoke, but only in a low whisper, in order not to distract the great conductor in his contemplations.

'No, no. Not Norway, old boy. *Sweden.*'

Jan Leeming
Television Presenter

A great number of people are not aware that those of us who work in broadcasting are freelance. Even though we might be 'part of the scenery', so to speak, and we may be with a television company for a long time, most of us work on contracts of between six months and a year.

I had had a very happy sojourn at HTV West in Bristol. I had been there for six years co-presenting the nightly news programme and I also had my own women's magazine programme called 'Women Only'. However, one has to move onwards and upwards and I had to make a move and decided to go to the magazine programme 'Pebble Mill' at the BBC in Birmingham.

I have a friend who lives near Stroud and she has a gardener, and being a Gloucestershire man he has quite an accent. I was very fortunate in that the West Country people had taken me to their heart and indeed were very fond of me. So when I decided to leave it made the local news. Apparently my friend's gardener came running up the path shouting:

'Ms. Neville, Ms. Neville, Jan Leeman's gone free range!'

The Rt. Hon. Viscount Leverhulme of the Western Isles

T.D.

Past Chancellor of Liverpool University
Lord-Lieutenant of the City and County of Chester

My story concerns two Lancashire men.

The first man: 'Lend me a lantern.'

The second man: 'What do you want a lantern for?'

The first man: 'I am going courting.'

The second man: 'I never took a lantern when I went courting.'

The first man: 'I thought not when I saw your wife.'

The Lord Lloyd of Kilgerran
C.B.E., Q.C., J.P.

Past Chairman, Foundation of Science and Technology

When referring to the small number of women involved in the civic life of the City of London

Heinrich Heine, the German poet, many years ago was asked:
'Where would you like to be when the end of the world comes and all is destroyed?'
His answer was: 'I would like to be in England.'
When asked why in England, he said: 'Everything happens in England usually fifty years after it has happened everywhere else!'

Christopher Logue
Writer, Playwright, Composer and Actor

I was told the following story about Victor Passmore, the painter.

Picasso agreed to open the I.C.A. in – when was it? – '52, '53? – no matter. An hour before his train was due to arrive, the late Roland Penrose, first president of the I.C.A., realised that no one had been detailed to meet him at Victoria Station. After a few telephone calls Victor Passmore was given the honour. Reaching the station and seeing the great man coming down the platform, Victor Passmore remembered that he did not speak French and guessed, correctly, that Picasso would not speak English.

Mute introductions and smiles covered their finding a taxi, but once inside, silence fell. After a minute, Victor Passmore, summoning up his French, said, 'Moi, je suis peintre.' To which Picasso replied, 'Moi aussi.'

The Rt. Hon. The Countess of Longford

C.B.E.

Author

The following anecdote occurs in a book by Sir Charles Petrie on the Victorian Age.

Gladstone once taunted a certain Father Healy about a local Italian priest who was offering to rescue souls from Purgatory at 25 lire a time.

'I ask you, as a clergyman of the Church of Rome,' said Gladstone, 'what have you to say to that?' Gladstone, of course, was an ardent Anglican.

Father Healy replied, 'Tell me of any other Church, Mr. Gladstone, that would do it at that price.'

The Rt. Hon. The Earl of Longford

K.G., P.C.

Writer

A funny thing happened to me on my way to this dinner. I walked through a graveyard and on one of the tombstones I saw inscribed:

'Here Lies (*fill in name*), an estate agent (*politician, journalist, banker or whatever*) and an honest man.'

I said to myself, 'That's the first time I have ever come across two men buried in the same grave.'

Admiral Sir Raymond Lygo

K.C.B.

Managing Director, British Aerospace

The best stories after dinner are those which fit in neatly with the general remarks and always have to have some particular relevance to the occasion. The only kind that I know sometimes will work are anecdotal, and one of the only advantages of getting older is that your store of anecdotes becomes greater, in fact you enter your anecdotage.

Some years ago when I had completed my time as Captain of the *Ark Royal*, I was asked by their Lordships, I now realise almost in desperation because they could not think of anything else for me to do, to start a team to tour the country which was called the Naval Presentation Team. I believe it still continues to exist. The object was to talk to the influential opinion-formers in the country, to get across the naval message. The show lasted about forty-five minutes and consisted of a mixture of live appearances by Lygo, mixed in with film appearances by Lygo and a great deal of footage on naval events.

As part of the procedure, we decided to try a couple of down-market appearances as well as up-market, to see how the message would be taken. One of these was at a local Rotarians gathering. By this time I was getting a somewhat overrated sense of my own importance, because the press coverage had been fairly extensive and everything had gone extremely well. This occasion was the only one which my wife attended and she sat next to our host.

During the course of dinner, he asked her, "Ow long is Captin's speech?' My wife replied, 'About forty-five minutes including a film.' A stunned look passed over the Chairman's face: 'Forty-five minutes!'

There was a long pause, and as we had now approached the end of the formal repast, he proceeded as follows. Seizing the gavel he struck it with a large blow, leapt to his feet and said: 'Laddes and Gentilmen, the Queen.' This was followed immediately by another large crash on the gavel, whereupon he announced solemnly: 'Owing to the fact that the Captin's speech will last for forty-five minutes, I can only allow you five minutes to relieve yourselves!'

The thought passed through my mind that if in fact he was concerned about the length of the speech perhaps he should have provided a longer pause before I started! Nevertheless, after the scramble for the door, and the subsequent re-entry, we were ready to start my speech. With a resounding crash on the gavel the Chairman stood up:

'Laddes and Gentilmen, I 'ave much pleasure in introdoosing to you the whirld famus Captin Lid.'

Ah well, when it comes to public speaking, sometimes you win and sometimes you lose!

The Rt. Hon. The Lord Mackay of Clashfern
Past Lord Chancellor

The Honourable Lord Cameron, father of the present Lord Advocate, was until his retirement a very distinguished judge of the Scottish Court of Session. On one occasion, when introducing a brother judge to a student law society, he was heard to say:

'He is an excellent judge. You don't have to tell him everything seven times before he takes it in – five times is generally quite sufficient.'

The Rt. Hon. Lord Marshall of Leeds
Politician

Official Gobbledegook

In a case where a scheme (*the first scheme*) was an
earner's chosen scheme on the date with effect from
which the first scheme ceased to be an appropriate
scheme, the date specified in a notice under section 1(9)
as the date from which another scheme (*the second
scheme*) is to be the earner's chosen scheme may be the
date with effect from which the first scheme ceased to be
an appropriate scheme (whether or not that date is 6th
April), if that date is not earlier than whichever is the
earlier of –
(*a*) the date 6 months earlier than that on which the
     Secretary of State receives the notice, and
(*b*) 6th April in the tax year in which the Secretary of
     State receives the notice.

(The above is taken from a Paper of the D.H.S.S. dated
November 1986 and entitled 'Reforming Social Security'.)

*   *   *

Burnham Category II/III courses may or may not be
advanced and poolable. A Burnham Category II/III course
which is not poolable is not poolable only because it is
not advanced, i.e. it does not require course approval as
an advanced course. It is therefore wrong to describe it as
a 'non-poolable advanced (non-designated) course'. Non-
poolable courses are non-advanced by definition. I think
that the problem you have described probably results
from confusion here.

(The above emanated from the D.E.S., in a letter they
sent to teachers' pay negotiators.)

His Excellency The Hon. Mr. Douglas McClelland

A.C.

Past Australian High Commissioner

When Her Majesty the Queen was about to pay her first visit to Australia in 1954, arrangements were being made for Her Majesty to visit one of Australia's large industrial centres.

The mayor and officials of the City gave consideration to how the City could best honour the occasion of the Royal visit and eventually recommended a new chandelier be purchased for the foyer of the Council Chambers. After the mayor had put his recommendation to the Council, the subject was thrown open for debate.

One of the Aldermen sprang to his feet. 'Mr. Mayor,' he said, 'I strongly oppose your proposal. I don't think you and your officers have researched the matter sufficiently Although I do not have any detailed knowledge of the cost, nonetheless I think it is a shocking waste of taxpayers' money because in all the years that I have lived in this great city, frankly I can't remember having met one person who can play such an instrument. The Council would be far better off buying a piano.'

His Excellency Mr. Roy McMurtry

Q.C.

Past Canadian High Commissioner

My story is simply about a political speaker who is asked to address a distinguished audience for a very specified, i.e. brief, period of time. However, the political speaker, apparently under some delusions of eloquence, rambles on long beyond the allotted time frame. As the audience becomes restless and somewhat hostile, the frustrated Chairman of the meeting, not being able to take it any longer, reaches over and picks up the toastmaster's wooden gavel and takes a swipe at the political speaker.

Fortunately, or unfortunately, it misses, but descends squarely on the head of the person who is sitting on the other side of the speaker. As that gentleman slides under the table, he is heard to say, 'Hit me again, I can still hear him.'

Sir Yehudi Menuhin

K.B.E.

Violinist, Conductor and Author

One day in summer, many years ago, I hailed a taxi to Portland Place to go back to our house in Highgate Village, a good thirty minutes' drive.

The first taxi that stopped said: 'No, no, it was too far away.' After a long wait, the second taxi came along and he said: 'No, no, it was time for his lunch.'

At that time I did not realise that the passenger had to put a foot inside the door, after which the driver must take him to wherever he wanted to go. I have never put a foot inside the door without being asked, but such courtesies are obviously out of date.

Finally, the third taxi came along and he declined with some excuse, probably hoping I'd offer him a double fare, and as I walked away he shouted:

'Has anyone ever told you how much shorter you look off stage?'

* * *

To do the taxi drivers justice, however, I will relate another incident. A few weeks later I got into a taxi and, as usual, discovered I had no money. However, on the long trip to Highgate we engaged in conversation, and he told me about his daughter's love of music and that she played the oboe. I invited the family to my next concert, which was to be a few days later.

When I finally arrived at my home in Highgate, the taxi driver refused payment of any kind, saying it had been his pleasure, and thus saving me my usual request for money from my housekeeper.

Lady Mills (Mary Hayley Bell)
Author and Playwright

Late one evening, when a dinner party was just finishing and the guests were gathered in the hall saying goodbye, a small figure in a long white nightdress appeared at the top of the stairs. It was my daughter Hayley, aged five.

During a moment of startled silence she looked straight at me and said very calmly and quietly, 'Mummy, my heart has stopped.'

Sheridan Morley
Author, Journalist and Broadcaster

I do rather cherish the memory of two ladies sitting in front of me at Stratford-on-Avon years ago, in the days when the theatre there still had a curtain which used to come down to tell you when the play was over.

On that occasion, it was a long and very bloody *Antony and Cleopatra* and, as the curtain very slowly descended on the usual last-act array of Shakespearian corpses (Cleopatra, Charmian, Iras), one of the ladies turned and said in ringing tones:

'The very same thing, dear, happened to Maureen.'

Sometimes I still worry about that.

Malcolm Muggeridge
Broadcaster and Author

We were living in a house on the shore of Salt Spring Island in Canada, overlooking a stretch of water separating us from Vancouver Island.

One day, I saw on the beach a beautiful white seagull standing on a rock with a broken wing. As I looked, a large baldheaded crow swooped down from above and attacked the wounded bird viciously, pecking him with his sharp beak. Then as I looked, I became aware of two beautiful white seagulls flying over the water towards the shore. Landing on the beach, they at once came to the rescue of their wounded brother, attacking the crow until he flew off to where he had come from. Then they remained standing guard over their wounded friend until he died.

This seemed to me to be one of nature's parables, telling us to help our fellows who are suffering from the vicious jabs of cancer.

The Rt. Rev. Peter Mumford
Bishop of Truro

I had been asked to be the Speaker at an important
luncheon in the City of London. I was warned that the
Lord Mayor would have to leave promptly at a certain
time for a Royal engagement, and that although I could
expect to be called not later than five minutes past two
o'clock, I must stop at 2.15 p.m. without fail.

There was a large clock opposite the top table which
duly registered 2.05 when I stood up to speak. After only
two minutes, however, the toastmaster tapped my
shoulder and told me to stop immediately.

'But you said I'd got until quarter past,' I whispered,
although all could hear over the public address system.

'I know,' hissed the toastmaster, 'the clock stopped.'

His Excellency Señor Navarrete
Past Mexican Ambassador

God, in His wisdom, decided to speak directly with three Heads of State, giving them the opportunity to seek His guidance about the greatest problem each of them was facing. Each of them was only allowed one question. First, the President of the Federal Republic of Germany asked:

'Will my country ever be reunited?'

'Yes,' was the answer, 'but not during your time in office, my son.'

Immediately after, the King of Spain was received, and he asked:

'Will we be able to cope successfully with ETA's terrorism?'

'Yes, my son,' came the answer, 'but not during your reign.'

Finally, the Brazilian President was admitted to His presence. He asked:

'Will the debt problem be resolved?'

'Yes, my son,' God replied, 'but not during *my* reign.'

*   *   *

This story was overheard during a dinner soon after my arrival in England. The subject being discussed was the quality of restaurants in London. While one of them was stressing the excellence of London restaurants, the other remained rather sceptical and asked for clarification.

'To which very good restaurants are you referring?' he asked.

'Well,' came the answer, 'there are top-notch ethnic restaurants.'

'Really? Which one, for instance?'

'Well, of course, Simpson's in the Strand.'

Sir Angus Ogilvy
Past President of the Imperial Cancer Research Fund

My father was a lovely man, but sadly – in the latter part of his life – he could, on occasions, become quite irascible. I shall never forget coming down to breakfast one morning to find him fuming over some leading article which had appeared in *The Scotsman*. It was shortly after Roy Thompson had taken it over. I did my best to persuade my father not to ring up Roy personally and tell him exactly what he thought of it. Once a decision was taken, however, my father was not a man to be deflected.

So he rang at about 8.45 in the morning and was put through to Roy's secretary. She was a very Scottish lady, and I think must have sensed danger because she gave a somewhat evasive reply. My father, whose name was Lord Airlie, thought it might help if he told her who he was.

'I am Airlie,' he said.

'So what?' retorted the girl. 'I'm early too.'

The Rt. Hon. Sir Michael Palliser

G.C.M.G, P.C.

Diplomat

A Soviet citizen had at last, after a long wait, been told that he could buy the small car he had been interested in. When he called on the dealer he was assured that he could take delivery of the car – but in ten years' time.

'Excellent,' he said. 'Would that be in the morning or the afternoon?'

The dealer asked in some surprise why he needed to know this, given that the car would not be available for ten years.

'Ah,' the Soviet purchaser replied, 'but you see, I have the plumber coming in the morning!'

His Excellency Mr. Ilkka Pastinen
The Finnish Ambassador, 1983–91

A man was flying in a hot air balloon, when the weather got suddenly darker. He decided to get lower in order to find a landmark. There was no landmark, only a man walking his dog on the moor.

'Hello, there!' bellowed the man in the balloon. 'Can you tell me where I am?'

'You are in a hot air balloon, about 200 yards above the ground,' shouted the man below.

'Are you, by any chance, a diplomat?' asked the man in the balloon.

'Yes, I am,' said the man on the ground. 'How did you guess?'

'Because diplomats are people full of useless information,' said the man in the balloon.

The Rt. Hon. The Lord Ponsonby of Shulbrede
Opposition Chief Whip, House of Lords

An experience I recall which sometimes bears repeating, is when I was speaking at an American travel agents' dinner and the toastmaster announced the toast of the Queen. My neighbour immediately grabbed me in frantic excitement, clutched my arm and asked, 'Is she coming?' I assured her that she was not, that this was a form of toast we had in this country.

It took some time for her excitement to subside, but later she told me that it wasn't quite such a fanciful question, as when she had attended a dinner in Washington some years previously the President had been announced and Lyndon Johnson had just walked in.

His Excellency Mr. Charles H. Price II
Past United States Ambassador

Benjamin Franklin served as a delegate to the
Constitutional Convention in Philadelphia during the
summer of 1787. Although an elderly man, he worked
hard throughout the day. To reward himself, he would
spend his evenings in merriment at a local tavern.

It seems that another delegate, who abstained from
strong drink himself and frowned on those who
indulged, resolved to give Franklin an object lesson in
clean living.

One day, the teetotaller brought in two clear glasses
and two worms. He put one worm in a glass of water,
where it began to swim. He put the other in a glass of
rum, whereupon it died instantly.

'Now, Mr. Franklin, what does that teach you?' he
asked.

Franklin replied, 'If you have worms, drink rum.'

The Rt. Hon. Lord Prior

P.C.

Past Lord President of Council and Leader of the House of Commons
Past Secretary of State for Northern Ireland

I really like the one about the Irishman who put in his will that he should be buried at sea, and three Irishmen were drowned digging the grave!

*   *   *

A true story is that when visiting South Armagh, I asked the local policeman how things were.

'Well,' he said, 'in this part they are all nationalists and would like to see a united Ireland, just so long as they could keep the border.'

Steve Race

F.R.A.M., F.R.S.A.

Broadcaster, Musician and Author

The curious thing about after-dinner stories is that Top People tend to think of them as the sort of risqué stories one might tell after the ladies have departed, whereas the rest of us think an after-dinner story is something a speaker might tell in public. I can only contribute a personal memory which I have occasionally told as part of an after-dinner speech.

In the 'My Music' TV and radio programme, for which I act as chairman and question-setter, I once asked my panellists to give an impromptu suggestion as to what might make an appropriate registration number for a musician's car.

Denis Norden thought that Johann Strauss's car might have been registered 123, 123; and Vincent Youman's car would, of course, be T 4 2.

John Amis suggested that a pianist specialising in Mozart concertos might enjoy having a car with the number K.488.

For a fiddle player, Frank Muir suggested V 10 LIN.

But Denis mystified us all by proposing a car number for Wagner, which he insisted should be 9 W.

'Why?' I asked, obligingly.

'It was the answer Wagner used to give,' said Denis, 'whenever anyone said to him, "Do you spell your name mit V?"'

Ronald Reagan

President of the United States, 1981–89

Remarks at the Conservative Political Action Conference,
thirteenth annual dinner, 30 January 1986

It reminds me of a favourite little story of mine about a
career naval officer who finally got his four stripes,
became a captain and then was given command of a giant
battleship. And one night he was out steaming around
the Atlantic when he was called from his quarters to the
bridge and told about a signal light in the distance. And
the captain told the signalman, 'Signal them to bear to
starboard.' And back came the signal from ahead asking
– or saying – '*You* bear to starboard.'

Well, as I say, the captain was very aware that he was
commander of a battleship, the biggest thing afloat, the
pride of the fleet and he said, 'Signal that light again to
bear to starboard *now*.' And, once again, back came the
answer, 'Bear to starboard yourself.'

Well, the captain decided to give his unknown
counterpart a lesson in seagoing humility; so he said,
'Signal them again and tell them to bear to starboard. I
am a battleship.'

And back came the signal, 'Bear to starboard yourself.
I'm a lighthouse.'

*   *   *

Remarks at a dinner for the Congressional leadership, 10 March 1986

Senator Majority Leader and Mrs. Secretary of Transportation Dole – I managed that one – Republican Leader Michel and Senators and Members of the House and ladies and gentlemen, having been on the mashed potato circuit in an earlier life, I know the danger of before-dinner speeches. Of course, there are pitfalls for every speaker.

You know, there was a young minister, and one day he was asking for a little sympathy from an older, more experienced minister, when he said that some of those hot, summer Sundays he would look out while he was preaching his sermon and the congregation would seem to be dozing off. And the older preacher said, 'Well, I know, I've had that experience, but,' he said, 'I found an answer to it.'

He said, 'When that begins to happen in the middle of your sermon, you just interrupt and say, "I want you all to know that last night I held in my arms a woman who was another man's wife." And,' he said, 'that'll wake them up. And then,' he says, 'you say to them, "And that woman was my dear mother."'

Well, time went by, and sure enough there was a Sunday and the young preacher was going at it. But they were beginning to doze off, and the kids were writing notes to each other and some of the women were knitting, but mainly they were dozing off. And he remembered what he'd been told, so he said, 'I want you all to know that last night I held in my arms a woman who was another man's wife.'

And suddenly, he was facing all those staring eyes and everyone was awake. And he tried to continue and he said, 'And that woman . . . I forget who she was.'

*   *   *

*Remarks at the Conservative Political Action Conference
luncheon, 20 February 1987*

You know, these last several weeks, I've felt a little bit
like that farmer that was driving his horse and wagon to
town for some grain and had a head-on collision with a
truck. And later was the litigation involving claims for his
injuries, some of them permanent. And he was on the
stand and a lawyer said to him, 'Isn't it true that while
you were lying there at the scene of the accident,
someone came over to you and asked you how you were
feeling, and you said you never felt better in your life?'
And he said, 'Yes, I remember that.'
Well, later, he's on the stand and the witnesses were
there – the lawyer for the other side is questioning – and
he said, 'When you gave that answer about how you felt,
what were the circumstances?'
'Well,' he said, 'I was lying there and a car came up
and a deputy sheriff got out.' He said, 'My horse was
screaming with pain – had two broken legs. The deputy
took out his gun, put it in the horse's ear and finished
him off. And,' he said, 'my dog was whining with pain –
had a broken back. And he went over to him and put the
gun in his ear. And then,' he says, 'he turned to me and
says, "Now, how are you feeling?"'

* * *

*Toast at a dinner honouring the National Governors'
Association, 22 February 1987*

It's been a pleasure to have met with you this evening
and to have had this opportunity to break bread and to
get to know you. Pardon me, but the circumstances
remind me a bit of the story of the Christians in
ancient Rome who were thrown into the arena there.
And moments later, why, the hungry lions were

released and came charging out at them. And before they could quite get at them, one of the Christians stood up, stepped forward, and said something. And the lions suddenly just laid down and refused to attack the Christians.

Well, the crowd at the Coliseum got mad. They yelled at the lions. They were throwing rocks at them and everything, but they couldn't get them to eat the Christians.

Finally, Nero called the Christian leader to his side and said, 'What is it that you told the lions?'

He said, 'I simply told them there would be speeches after the meal.'

The Lord Renton

P.C., K.B.E., Q.C., M.A., B.C.L., D.L.

A Deputy Speaker of the House of Lords since 1982

The Bishop was giving away the prizes at a girls' school. When he had given a prize to one of the senior girls who was about to leave the school, he asked her, 'What are you going to do when you leave school?'

She replied, 'I *was* going straight home, but why do you ask?'

*   *   *

Do you know the difference between a good barrister and a good surgeon?

It is that a good barrister never leaves anything out.

Brian Rix

C.B.E., M.A., D.U. (Essex)

Actor-Manager
Secretary-General of Mencap

Once upon a time there was a famous theatrical couple
who, when our story begins, were making their respective
ways up the ladder of success and were idyllically married.
One day the wife rushed into her husband's dressing room
as he was preparing for the evening performance.

'Oh, darling,' she said, 'I have just come from the press
show of your new film. Darling, it was fantastic! The
critics actually stood at the end and cheered! No one has
ever seen anything like it before. Imagine, darling – the
critics cheering! Oh, it was magnificent, darling. The most
exciting moment of my life. Oh, how I wished you'd been
there, for it was your performance they were cheering, my
darling. Your performance. The film itself was good, too,
but you were miraculous! The artistic merit and truth
behind the author's words were there for all to see, of
course. The costumes were magnificent. The direction –
faultless. The lighting and make-up *sans pareil*. There was
one tiny moment when you appeared to have no lips – but
that was nothing. Oh, my darling, you are going to be a
great star, probably the greatest star in all the theatrical
firmament and if my being with you should in any way
impede your meteoric rise, then I must leave you, my
darling, for it would be wrong of me to stand in the way of
one who is destined to straddle the world like a Colossus,
hear the thunder of applause from countless international
audiences, be showered with blandishments from all the
critics and receive the just financial rewards for one who is
truly great. So, choose, my darling, and if it be your wish
that you make your way like some mythical deity – lonely
but unencumbered – then you have only to say the word
and I will go through that door never to impose myself on
your dear life again.'

Came the reply, 'Yes, yes, yes. What do you mean, no
lips?'

Samuel Sheppard

O.B.E.

A distinguished elder of the City of London

This is a True Story ex Sheppard Family.

When my Grandmother died at ninety-eight, I was the one in the family responsible for the funeral. It was the united opinion that she wouldn't want to be buried with those new-fangled motors (this was about fifty years ago), so the undertaker was informed that it had to be horses (they and the carriages were a motley lot).

One of my cousins (Cicely) was in the Co-optomists as the Soubrette, so couldn't come, but her mother, Aunty Polly, in the twenty stone region, sat opposite me in the small carriage.

In the Roman Road our horse fell down and lay in the road. Mr. English, the undertaker, arrived, looked at the horse, said, 'Pick him up, put him in the hearse, it won't matter if he falls down there, and put the horse from the hearse in this one,' and we continued to the City of London cemetery in this fashion.

The Rt. Hon. Sir Greville Spratt

G.B.E., T.D., D.L.

Past Sheriff of the City of London, 1984–85
Lord Mayor of London, 1987–88

A True Story

An Irishman was up before the Bench for somewhat surprisingly stealing a large household gas meter, and had been apprehended by an alert young P.C. who saw him staggering out of a pub with it.

When asked to give his reasons for such an obvious theft, the accused replied, 'Well, your Honour, it was like this. I was asked by this smart boy in the bar would I like to buy the newest type of transistor radio complete with all the latest dials for a fiver. I thought it seemed a good buy.'

Sir Sigmund Sternberg
Kt., J.P., F.R.S.A., K.C.S.G.
Chairman, International Council of Christians and Jews

Jake said to Becky one day, 'Becky, I'm getting on in years and I can no longer live a lie. I must tell you that I have had a girl friend for quite some time now. What are you going to do about that?'

Becky considered carefully. The children were grown and married. She had a trust fund in her own name that gave her absolute security. Jake had been a good husband, and their marriage had been a comfortable one. She was no longer captivated by sex, and it was rather a relief to have someone else take over the responsibility.

So she said, 'Jake, if that's how it is, let it be. I won't interfere. As long as you keep up appearances and don't shame me before the neighbours and before my relatives, I will not object.'

Jake found this delightful, and life went on swimmingly. Several weeks later, he and Becky were in a restaurant and Jake waved at someone before sitting down.

Becky said, 'Whom are you waving at, Jake?'

Jake said, 'Do you see the blonde girl in the corner? That's my mistress. And the brunette girl next to her happens to be the mistress of my partner, Max.'

Becky looked, sank back in her chair, and said, 'You know, Jake, of the two, ours is much prettier.'

The Rt. Hon. Earl of Stockton

Chairman, Macmillan Publications, 1980–90
President of the London Europe Society

As a young man, I had the privilege of watching some of
the great post-war politicians from close quarters when
they visited my late Grandfather, then Harold Macmillan,
in Sussex. One of these was the late General de Gaulle.

I remember the final preparations for that great man's
visit to us in Sussex. My Grandmother bustled in and
announced crossly, 'Harold, I've just been rung up by a
young man from the Foreign Office who wants to know
where we are going to put the General's blood.'

My Grandpa took a moment to digest this, and who
wouldn't? 'My dear,' he replied, in his most reasoned
and reasonable voice, 'why have we got to put it
anywhere? Doesn't he keep it in his veins like other
mortals?'

It transpired that the French President had a very rare
blood group – not surprisingly when you think about it –
he couldn't have had a common one. At any rate, in view
of the ever-present risk of assassination, there had to be a
supply at hand. This precious essence had to be kept
cool.

Clutching at straws, my Grandfather suggested that
the receptacle, suitably disguised to avoid arousing the
more hysterical members of the staff, should be placed in
the kitchen fridge.

'Good heavens, no,' cried my Grandmother. 'Cook will
give notice in an instant if she has to have human blood
in her fridge – and foreign human blood to boot.
Anyway, there's no room. It's full of sausages and
haddock and things for Monday's lunch.'

In the end, the Ministry of Works found a fridge. Of
course, the only plug that fitted was in the squash court.
And there it sat, solemnly guarded by a lugubrious
French security man, to avoid the risk of Anglo-Saxon
contamination.

The Rt. Rev. Mervyn Stockwood

D.D.

Bishop of Southwark, 1959–80

When your wife tries to make you help with the washing-up and throws you the dish cloth, pretend she's passed you a handkerchief. Blow your nose on it and pass it back.

Godfrey Talbot

L.V.O., O.B.E.

Author, Broadcaster, Lecturer and Journalist

A Catholic priest, who had become very deaf in advanced years, had formed the habit of asking those erring members of his flock who came to his enclosed stall to write their penitences on a slip of paper, instead of speaking them to him. The practice worked fairly well until one day when, after the Father had heard a heavily breathing man enter the visitor's side of the confessional and fumble for a few moments, a small crumpled sheet was passed through the curtain and into the old cleric's hand.

The confession read: 'Two cans of beans. Quarter ham. Cans of Coke. Four fish fingers. Eggs. Bread rolls. Toilet roll. Large coffee. Six bottles. Soap. Marge. Washing-up.'

The priest studied the notes for a puzzled minute or two, and then silently passed the slip back.

Suddenly, however, came an agonised shout from beside him: 'Mother of God, I've left my sins in Sainsbury's!'

*   *   *

In the Second World War, the Dutch had plans against invasion, and one unusual defence idea: blow gaps in canals and sea-walls to let in floods, which might at least delay the overwhelming *Wehrmacht* in its advance.

A cable, with that idea in mind, had come from Queen Wilhelmina, stubbornly still in The Hague. Winston – who sometimes uttered terrible puns and schoolboy cracks even at the darkest hours – looked at the S.O.S., declared that Wilhelmina must be got out before she was captured and asked that a reply be cabled to her; then, with a sudden grin, suggested that the signal to Holland should be signed 'W.C.' and should read:

'HOLD YOUR WATER TILL THE JERRIES COME.'

Entry in a schoolchildren's essay competition on the wedding of Prince Charles and Lady Diana Spencer

'The Prince went to St. Paul's in an open cart, but Dinah went in a first-class carriage . . . She, the bride, sparkled in her hair; the veil was held to her head by the Spencer *terror* . . . They both made mistakes when exchanging their *vowels* . . . When they had been made man and wife, they walked forward and the marriage was *consummated* in front of the high altar, by the Archbiship of Canterbury, followed by several of London's top clergy . . . Back at the Palace, they waved to the crowds from the garage roof . . . They had lunch, called the Wedding Breakfast, of all things . . . After, they departed by balloons for their honeymoon at Broadmoor.'

*   *   *

Schoolboy Howlers

'Agricola? It was a soft drink for farm workers.'

'A brunette? A young bear.'

'We've been singing a hymn about an animal.'
  'What animal?'
  'A bear called Gladly . . . Gladly, the cross-eyed bear.'

'Nostalgia is Welsh for "Goodnight".'

Francis Drake (on Plymouth Hoe, told that the Spaniards were approaching): 'The Armada can wait, but my bowels can't.'

*   *   *

Notice in a bus in Guyana: 'Do not talk to driver or smoke or spit or swear.'

Notice in a foreign hotel bathroom: 'Visitors must not place strangers bodies in this lavatory.'

Notice in an elevator in a high-rise hotel in Japan (above the big panel of desired floor indicators): 'Please not to touch buttons which do not belong to you.'

Remark by a whirling-through-the-world American tourist leaving the Holy Land after a few hours there: 'I sure know now that Sodom and Gomorrah are *places* – not man and wife like Dan and Beersheba.'

A schoolboy, proud of his Latin-in-history, and flaunting *Honi soit qui mal y pense*, gave this splendidly free translation. It means: 'Honestly, sir, I think I'm going to be sick.'

* * *

My favourite tale of the famous wit, F. E. Smith, First Earl of Birkenhead, walking from the House of Commons with Labour's rough-hewn J. H. Thomas:

Says Jim: 'Oh, F. E., I've got an 'orrible 'ead.'

To which Lord Birkenhead's instant answer was: 'All you need take, my dear Jim, is a couple of aspirates.'

His Excellency Dr. Reginald Thomas

Austrian Ambassador Extraordinary and Plenipotentiary, 1982–88

Two delegates at an international conference were engaged in a lengthy debate on procedural matters, when a third delegate raised a point of order.

'Mr. Chairman,' he said, 'I have been listening to the debate between these two distinguished delegates with great attention. However, I cannot help being reminded in this context of two French cities – Toulon and Toulouse.'

At that, he sat down, and two minutes later the debate on procedural matters had ended.

The Rt. Hon. The Baroness Trumpington of Sandwich, in the County of Kent

A Baroness in Waiting (Government Whip)

When I was the Mayor of Cambridge I visited the National Stud in Newmarket. The Director told me I could safely go into any of the stallions' boxes. I was happily patting the stallion of my choice when rather strange things started to happen.

The Director put his head over the box and said, 'Are you wearing scent? Because if you are, you must come straight out of there. When the stallions aren't interested we put scent on the mares.'

Hurrying out of the box, I replied with as much dignity as I could muster: 'Not only am I wearing scent – but I am a Mayor.'

His Honour Judge Stephen Tumim
Circuit Judge and Author

Sir James Ingham at the age of seventy-one became Chief Metropolitan Magistrate in London, and he sat daily in that demanding office until he died at the age of eighty-five. One day he had before him at Bow Street two angry men. The complainant had been travelling on the old South-Western railway from Bournemouth to London. There were no corridors to the carriages, and he travelled alone to Basingstoke, where the defendant came into his compartment. The complainant dozed until Vauxhall, woke up, felt across his waistcoat and found his watch and chain were missing. The defendant was reading the newspaper.

Complainant: 'Has anyone else entered this compartment while I have been asleep?'

Defendant: 'No.'

Complainant: 'Then, sir, I must request you to tell me what you have done with my watch. It has been stolen during the time that you have been in the carriage. You had better return it, or I shall have to give you in charge on our arrival at Waterloo.'

The defendant was indignant, but at Waterloo a porter was sent to fetch a constable and the defendant was brought at once before Sir James, who asked the complainant if he had seen any other man come near the defendant at Waterloo.

Complainant: 'Yes, another man came up, apparently to enquire what was the matter.'

Sir James: 'Just so. That accounts for the disappearance of the watch. These things are never done alone – wherever a theft takes place, whether in a train, a crowd, or elsewhere, there is always a confederate to receive the stolen property. Prisoner, you are remanded for a week; but if you are a respectable man, I have no objection to take very substantial bail.'

The defendant's indignation burst out. He had just

come from years of foreign travel, he could find no friend to put up bail, he was being imprisoned without trial. Sir James was prevailed on to hear the case next day.

In the morning it was the complainant, and not the defendant, who spoke.

Complainant: 'I do not know how to express my regret for what has occurred. I find I did not lose my watch after all. I communicated my loss by telegraph to my wife at Bournemouth, and she has written to say that my watch and chain are safe at home. I dressed hurriedly to catch my train. I must have entirely forgotten to take my watch from the dressing-table.'

Sir James's wisdom was adaptable to the new facts. *He* had not spent the night in jail.

Sir James: 'It is a most remarkable occurrence. To show, however, how liable we all are to make these mistakes, I may mention, as an extraordinary coincidence, that I myself have only this morning been guilty of precisely the same oversight. I was under the impression, when I left my house at Kensington, that I put my watch (which, I may mention, is an exceedingly valuable one) in my pocket; but on arriving at this court, I found that I must have left it at home by mistake.'

The defendant was discharged amid much apologising from the complainant and much worldly smiling from the bench, although Sir James was less amused to find that the prisoner in the next case was absent. He completed his day's work and returned to Kensington, where his daughter met him in the drawing-room.

Miss Ingham; 'Papa, dear, I suppose you got your watch all right?'

Sir James: 'Well, my dear, as a matter of fact I went out this morning without it.'

Miss Ingham: 'Yes, I know papa, but I gave it to the man from Bow Street who called for it.'

Alan Whicker
Television Broadcaster and Writer

The joy of sea travel, of course, is that you can take all the luggage you like, without having to pack or unpack. On our *QE2* world cruise, the couple in the next stateroom bought so many hefty souvenirs – Thai teak furniture, Rajasthani chests, Balinese ebony statues – that their double cabin was jammed deck-to-ceiling with crates. They could only just squeeze into one of the beds, in a corner. She told me it was the first time they had slept together for years. Some women will do *anything* to go shopping . . .

*　　　*　　　*

As is legendary afloat, the menus are long, lavish and well-read. Shipboard meals are major events on the daily programme and all cruisers concentrate upon the serious business of masticating their moneysworth.

I heard two Indonesian stewards having a vicious row: 'And what's more,' snarled one, delivering the coup de grace, 'you eat like a *passenger* . . .'

Mrs. Mary Whitehouse
C.B.E.

Past President, National Viewers' and Listeners'
Association
Freelance Journalist, Broadcaster and Author

I don't think either of us have ever been so frightened in
our lives! My husband and I were on holiday visiting
relatives in Kenya, and our nephew took us for a visit to
the Game Reserve.

Because he knew the area so well he was allowed to
drive our jeep off the beaten track. About lunch time we
stopped at the end of a most beautiful water hole,
covered in water lilies on which exotic birds strutted and
sang.

After a while we decided to continue our journey but –
disaster! – the engine would not start! There we were,
miles and miles from civilisation, the only sight of which
were vehicles far away on the horizon, and far beyond
the sound of our voices or the car horn. There we were –
wild animals roaming around us, with no hope of being
found. At one point we saw a plane circling around
above and waved desperately, without effect.

After several hours – we had nothing to eat or drink! –
our nephew decided that the only hope was for him to
leave us where we were and set out to find help. The
hours passed and as we both sat there in the midst of the
vast expanse, silent except for the sound of the occasional
bird or animal, we could not help but wonder whether
indeed help would come in time.

Then my husband broke the silence. 'Don't move,' he
said, 'but there's a herd of elephants coming on the path
to the water, and we're in the way.' I had a mental
picture of our – frail, by elephants' standards! – vehicle
being swept into the lake, amongst the crocodiles. He
went on: 'There's only one thing to do – we must pray

that the Lord will turn them aside.' That we did and, as we watched them draw nearer and nearer, we saw them gradually change direction and pass us – very close! – by.

What an answer to prayer that was. And, incidentally, our nephew arrived a couple of hours later, complete with a team to heave us out and take us back to civilisation just as night was falling!

Colin Wilson
Author

A married woman, who suffered from appalling headaches, heard about a new doctor who specialised in hypnosis and auto-suggestion. She went to see him and returned in a highly indignant state of mind.

'The man is a total fraud. He told me that all I have to do is sit down on the edge of the bed, place both hands against my forehead and repeat over and over again: "I have not got a headache, I have not got a headache." '

A few weeks later, when her husband received a bill from the doctor, she told him not to pay it. Her husband asked if she had tried the treatment, and when she admitted that she hadn't, said that she ought to do so before he refused to pay the bill.

To her amazement, it worked marvellously. From then on, she was able to control all her headaches. The husband paid the bill immediately.

Some time later, the husband began to suffer from depression and sexual impotence. His wife suggested that he should go and see the same doctor. It worked like magic – her husband became a satyr in bed. But when she asked him about the doctor's advice, he was extremely evasive. However, he always insisted on going to bed ten minutes before she did, and one night she crept up to the bedroom door and put her eye to the keyhole. Her husband was sitting on the edge of the bed, with both hands pressed against his forehead, repeating, 'She is not my wife, she is not my wife.'

The Rt. Hon. The Lady Wilson of Rievaulx
Author and Poet

When my husband was Prime Minister, he gave a very long interview to Alistair Burnet. This was held at Chequers. The subjects discussed ranged over home affairs and world affairs, and it lasted for an hour and went out at peak viewing-time.

A few days later I received the following letter from a woman viewer:

Dear Mrs. Wilson

I saw your husband recently being interviewed by Alistair Burnet. That was a very nice chair he was sitting on! I hoped he would get up and walk about a bit, so that I could have a better look at it, but unfortunately he didn't. The material covering the chair is just what I need for my new drawing-room curtains – would you please tell me where you bought it, and how much it cost?

I wonder how much of the interview she heard? Which only proves that you can take a horse to the water, but you can't make him or her drink!